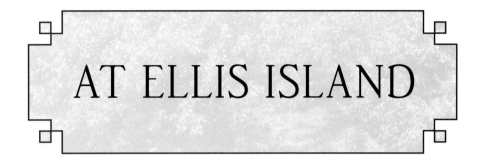

AT ELLIS ISLAND

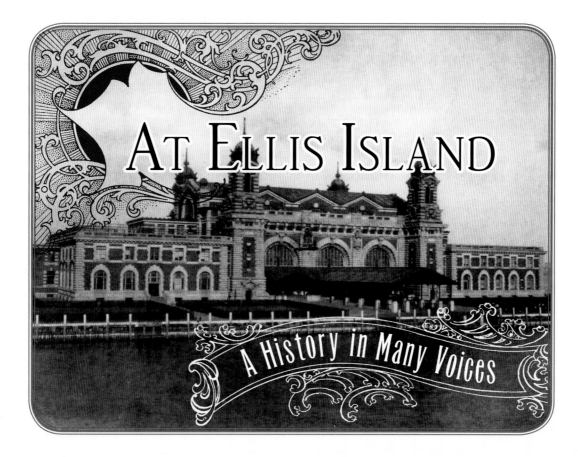

AT ELLIS ISLAND

A History in Many Voices

by LOUISE PEACOCK

Illustrated by WALTER LYON KRUDOP

Atheneum Books for Young Readers
New York   London   Toronto   Sydney

Atheneum Books for Young Readers

An imprint of Simon & Schuster Children's Publishing Division

1230 Avenue of the Americas

New York, New York 10020

Book design by Patti Ratchford

The text of this book is set in AT Burin Roman, Bureau Roxy Medium,
Carlton Plain, Colwell, CG Miehle Condensed, Della Robbia, Edwardian
Medium, Memimas, and P22 PanAm.

The illustrations for this book are rendered in gouache.

Manufactured in China

First Edition

10 9 8 7 6 5 4 3 2 1

Library of Congress Cataloging-in-Publication Data

Peacock, Louise.

At Ellis Island : a history in many voices / by Louise Peacock ; illustrated
by Walter Lyon Krudop.

p.   cm.

Summary: The experiences of people coming to the United States from many
different lands are conveyed in the words of a contemporary young girl
visiting Ellis Island and of a girl who immigrated in about 1910, as well as
by quotes from early twentieth-century immigrants and Ellis Island officials.

ISBN-13: 978-0-689-83026-6

ISBN-10: 0-689-83026-2

[1. United States—Emigration and immigration—Fiction. 2. Immigrants—
Fiction. 3. Ellis Island Immigration Station (N.Y. and N.J.)—Fiction.]

[I. Krudop, Walter, 1966– ill. II. Title.]

PZ7.P31173 At 2002

[Fic]—dc21   00-054281

Photo Credits:

The photographs on pages 2 and 40 are courtesy of Michael McCartney.
The photograph on page 17 (bottom right) is courtesy of Leslie's Weekly
(July 2, 1887). The photograph on page 20 (bottom) is courtesy of the
New York Public Library. All other photographs are courtesy of the
National Archives.

AUTHOR'S NOTE

Ellis Island was as much a surprise to me as it was to the thousands of immigrants who once passed through its doors. I'd never intended to visit the island. My children wanted to visit the Statue of Liberty, and when the ferry docked at Ellis Island, we decided to take a look around.

Ellis Island was an overwhelming experience. I've tried to show some of the awe and amazement that filled me in the narrative of the modern child visiting the island. I, too, traced the names carved in the Wall of Honor with my fingertip.

I was overwhelmed by the sight of the boxes, baskets, and bags in the Baggage Hall. What would it have felt like, I wondered, to step into the unknown, carrying a single suitcase? I was even more amazed at some of the answers I found to that question.

That's how I came to think of Sera. She is an imaginary character, but many of her experiences really did happen to someone. I hope you'll like her story.

There is an American flag here, in front of the tall windows. It curves, rippling in an imaginary breeze. As I walk past, it seems to ripple again, and bit by bit the red-and-white stripes disappear, replaced by faces, hundreds and hundreds of different faces.

Mama,

Today I am on the ship. I watched the harbor fall away behind us. I am safe. You were right. But oh, Mama, how I wish you were safe here with me.

I will not let myself remember my last sight of you. I will think only of your face, when we were safe at home together, when there was peace.

How could you stand it?" I asked a girl who had told a tale of war; of bombs dropping about her; of starvation; of the horrors of pogroms.

"We had hope," she said simply. "Without hope we would have died. . . . And see— we are here, my sister and I, in America. Now that we are with our father, we can begin again."
—C. Razovski, reporter

[The trip from Europe] was rough. The food was bad. You couldn't even eat at a table. We used to eat like beggars there, we ate sitting on the floor, with our plates next to us. White tin plates.
—Tessie Croce
arrived in America in 1912, age 15 ½

We spent eleven days on board ship. The first four days we were deathly sick, seasick, because we were down in the hold. The cheapest possible ticket . . . I was so sick, and I wanted to die. I was seven years old.
—Rota Fichbach
arrived from Germany in 1926, age 7

My father took me to the main street, and all the people that got killed, their bodies were piled up on the sidewalk. It was horrible. Blood all over. So my father says, "Well, there's no use staying here." . . . We went from Athens by boat to the Italian coast, and [there] they put us [on another boat] in the freight, in the hold. And we were lucky for that. We made it. It was like a barn down there. They had only cots. "You ought to be happy you're getting out alive," someone said.

—James Karavolas

arrived from Greece in 1915, age 6

Ah, you cannot believe how crowded we are here. We are in the very bottom of the ship, what they call steerage. No windows. No air. Row after row of bunk beds and everyone in them sick from the rolling of the ship. The woman in the next bunk, the one who is supposed to look after me, cannot raise her head. I think maybe she will die.

I am not sick. I go and run on the deck, breathe the fresh air. There is no smell of blood in the air here on the ocean.

Almost half of all Americans alive today had an ancestor who came through this place, Ellis Island. My grandmother's grandmother was one of them, almost a hundred years ago. She came in that great rush of immigrants that crowded through Ellis Island before World War I, when this huge brick building was only twenty years old.

After my father went to America in 1906, he was writing back to us and sending money. . . . Then he saved up money for the tickets to get us over here. He wanted his family. It took five years for him to save up enough money to take us over.
—Sonya Kevar
arrived from Russia in 1911, age 13

My father and I, we get up on the deck. . . . [A]nd then I left, and he was crying. And you know how I felt when I left my home, my father and my mother? Terrible, terrible. That's how I felt. I was the first in my family to come.
—Theodore Spako
arrived from Greece in 1911, age 16

Now the weather is clear and bright, and the ocean is calm. Everyone feels a little better. Even the woman in the next bunk came on deck to see the sun. One of the men started to play his harmonica, and some of us danced. I laughed for joy when I spun around.

There are so many of us here, people from all over. Some are very sad, very lonely, leaving all their families behind. Some are coming to join their family in America. They are the happiest, laughing.

Because of my great-great-grandmother, because of her bravery, I am an American. My face could be on this flag.

The people were all feeling lousy, scratching. They were dirty. They didn't get no attention. . . . When we got off the boat, got to Ellis Island, people were sitting on the benches scratching from the lice. They were loaded with lice.
—Jake Kreider
arrived from Austria in 1911, age 11

I remember the food was so bad that many times my mother would say, "Don't eat it." . . . We were allowed to go out on the deck. People from upstairs, first class and second class, would look down on us, and they would feel sorry for us, and many times they would throw down an orange, or apples, or candy.
—Esther Gidiwicz
arrived from Romania in 1905, age 5

The food is not very good. I eat it anyway, Mama. I think you would tell me to do that if you were here. We have tin plates. We can wash them after each meal, but there isn't much hot water, so it is hard. I can't wash myself, either. You would not like the way I look today, all dirty and my hair all tangled. I try the best I can. Watch over me, Mama.
Your loving daughter,
Sera

But what a leap into the unknown that was for her!

Dear Mama,

A terrible storm these three days. They drove us down into the hold and bolted the doors so we couldn't come up again. Everything roared down there, like the ocean itself was swallowing us. The ship rolled so hard, it knocked me out of my bed and I bruised myself on the floor. Everyone was crying and praying and screaming. I prayed to Our Father, the prayer you taught me. I guess he listened this time, because finally the ship stopped heaving. They opened the doors, and we could see sunlight again, the first in days. It made me blink and blink.

And what dangers she faced during the crossing!

The ship sprung a hole and water was coming in. In fact, we were walking around with our life jackets. They sent an SOS out, and told us another ship was coming to help us. . . . [I]n New York they reported in the paper that the *Mongolia* sunk, and all the people went down.
—Evelyn Berkowitz
arrived from Hungary in 1909, age 12

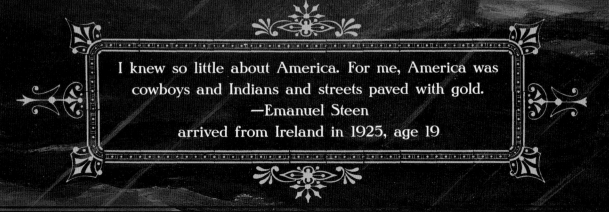

I knew so little about America. For me, America was cowboys and Indians and streets paved with gold.
—Emanuel Steen
arrived from Ireland in 1925, age 19

I look at the old boxes and trunks and baskets and bags stacked here, in the baggage room. Back then there would have been thousands of them piled here every day while the owners went upstairs to be examined, to find out if they could enter America.

Y ou should see all the kinds of people on that Ellis Island. . . . Oh, my Lord! I grew up on a farm in Europe and I wasn't used to this—but there you saw all kinds. Some of them looked like beggars—they were dressed in patches. Some of the men had big beards; and their hair, some of the Jewish people had braids. There were a lot of people, all kinds, and all of them seemed to me poorer looking and poorer dressed than I was. Some of them were very tragic, with patches one on top of another and the coats and suits. People looked ruined, as if they were coming from some kind of great poverty.

—Vera Gauditsa

arrived from Czechoslovakia in 1928

We picked up a little boat all full of people. Their ship sank in the storm. They looked tired, too tired to move, too tired to live maybe. One boy and girl were holding hands. They are from the same country and they met on the lifeboat. Both of their families drowned. They want to stay together now.

They each had had a little sister about my age. So they have taken me for a little sister and look after me. We sit on the deck together and talk about America, what it will be like. I tell them Papa did not come home to Armenia like Uncle Gregor but sent tickets for us, and now he is waiting for me in America.

ow strange it must have been to them—so many people, so many languages, so much confusion. How frightening it must have been. They traded information while they waited, of course. Friends who had come earlier had sent back reports. But these newcomers couldn't really know what was waiting for them.

At that time, somebody had to be responsible for you. My sister didn't know I was coming. If nobody's there [to claim you], you had to have twenty-five dollars on you. I didn't have it.
—Jacob Lotsky arrived from Ukraine in 1920, age 19

They say I am lucky Papa is waiting! If you
are a child alone, they won't let you in America.
Alberto and Rosa are sixteen. That's how old you
have to be to come in alone.

I hope they will be all right. Alberto taught
me to whistle with my fingers like he does. It is
a great loud sound! They have no money. I think
you have to have money to come to America.
Sera

Dear Mama,

This long voyage is over. We are in the harbor now. The land looks like mountains, but no snow! Alberto says they are tall buildings, the tallest in the world. Tomorrow we take the little boat to Ellis Island.

Oh, Mama, I saw the Lady. We all pushed and shoved to get where we could see her. She is so beautiful, with her crown and her torch held high. Her face looks like yours, Mama, so calm and kind. I wept with joy when I saw her.

My grandmother tells me her grandmother's stories—of crops trampled in the fields and starvation the following winter, of young men dragged away to serve in the armies. I can understand leaving that! Some of the immigrants had even darker stories, of blood running through the streets, of whole villages burned to the ground. Even the unknown would be better than that.

Gus ask me, "What's the statue?" And then we're looking at the statue, and his father say, "That's Christopher Columbus." And I put my two cents out. I say, "Listen, this don't look like Christopher Columbus. That's a lady there."
—Theodore Spako arrived from Greece in 1911, age 16

When we got to America, we saw the Statue of Liberty and Mother said to me, "That means we are free." I remember her saying that. And I didn't know what she meant by being "free." I only learned that after. And to this day I think I'm a better American than a lot of them born here, because when I sing "God Bless America," I'm in tears.
—Margaret Wertle arrived from Hungary in 1910, age 7

My grandmother's grandmother would have climbed these stairs, but then they would have been full of people, all wondering what would happen next. The inspectors watched the people climb the steps. Sometimes they put a chalk mark on an immigrant's coat. That person would be taken out of line.

As the immigrant approaches, the officer gives him a quick glance. Experience enables him in that one glance to take in six details, namely, the scalp, face, neck, hands, gait, and general condition, both mental and physical. Should any of these details not come into view, the alien is halted and the officer satisfies himself that no suspicion or symptom exists regarding that particular detail. . . .
—E. H. Mullan,
surgeon, U.S. Public Health Service

Suddenly, I saw an inspector marking a cross on my sleeve. I was wearing a coat, a blue overcoat; I saw that on me he had made a cross, but on someone else, no cross, and they were pushing the ones with a cross to one side and the rest to the other. I didn't know why he had put this cross on me, so I took off my coat and I put it over my arm and I kept going.
—Baruch Chasimov
arrived from Russia in 1909, age 25

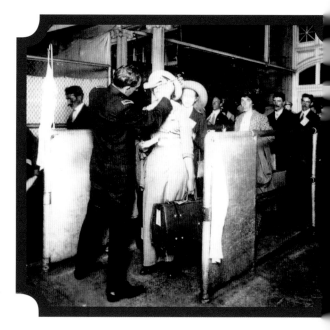

The little boat comes to a dock. They pin a number to my dress. Why do I wear a number? They have on uniforms like the soldiers at home. I am a little frightened, Mama. Look down on me here. Help me to be brave.

Hurry, hurry! We all rush to the big brick building. Some leave their boxes at the door, but I am carrying nothing. We walk up the big staircase in a line. The men in uniforms look hard at us as we walk by. Sometimes they make a mark on someone's coat.

They didn't know why. They didn't know the inspectors made a "seven second exam" to look for illness or deformity. They only knew some people were taken out of the line. Those people had a more complete examination. If they failed, they might be sent to the hospital for treatment, or they might be sent back to the ship, back where they came from.
Sent away from America.

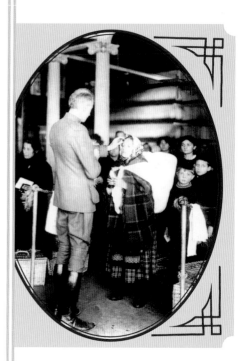

Now, after fifty-one years, I can't imagine what a job they had spelling all those names, all different nationalities—it's not so easy. Some of the names were so long, so hard to pronounce and hard to spell, and so I was always waiting to hear when they were going to call my name, if they could only spell it.
—Marta Forman
arrived from Czechoslovakia in 1922

What a place that was! Beautiful. Balconies on top, you know, all the way around, and people who had to wait a long time could go upstairs and watch the people downstairs.
—Bessie Spylios
arrived from Greece in 1909, age 11

I have never seen a room like this, Mama. It is bigger than a church. The high windows let the sun stream in on us. Beautiful! I just want to stare and stare. Such a place! But so much noise— I have never heard so many people talk at once, in all the languages there are.

At the top of the steps the immigrants entered the Registry Room, where they had to answer many questions. A redheaded girl wearing a long dress and speaking in a thick Irish brogue was the very first to come through here. Her name was Annie Moore. The year was 1892. To celebrate the occasion, the officials gave her a ten-dollar gold piece.

From nine o'clock in the morning to nine in the evening, we were continuously examining aliens. . . . Every twenty-four hours from three to five thousand people came before us, and I myself examined from four to five hundred a day. We were simply swamped by that human tide.
—Frank Martocci, interpreter, remembering conditions in 1907

In lines again, behind iron bars like cattle. We each wait to be questioned. The man sits like a judge, high up, high. He is in a uniform, like a soldier, but I can't see a sword or a gun. He speaks to me, but I don't know the words. He looks at the paper on his desk and frowns.

Another man comes over. "Where are you from, little girl?" he asks me. This one speaks Armenian, and I smile. He tells me the questions the man at the desk asks, and I answer them.

"How old are you?" he asks then.

I am frightened. I remember what Alberto said. "Sixteen!" I tell him.

The man looks at his paper again and frowns. I swallow hard and look away.

What is your name? they were asked. What is your nationality? How old are you? What is your final destination in the United States? Who paid for your ticket? Do you have any money? Have you ever been in prison or a poorhouse? What is the condition of your health?
Most immigrants answered about twenty questions before they were allowed to continue.

Another little sidelight on how an immigrant got through the lines here. Not all of it was done exactly the way the officials would like it to be, because $25 was not available to everybody as they arrived. I can assure you that certain $25s were passed along from one passenger to another to help out those that didn't have it, and this had to be done with a quick motion of the hand so no one would get caught doing this.
—Hans Bergner
arrived from Germany in 1924

LIST OR MANIFEST OF ALIEN IMMIGRANTS FOR THE COMMISSIONER OF IMMIGRATION

Required by the regulations of the Secretary of the Treasury of the United States, under Act of Congress approved March 3, 1893, to be delivered to the Commissioner of Immigration by the Commanding Officer of any vessel having such passengers on board upon arrival at a port in the United States.

In the next line are Alberto and Rosa.
"Do you have money?" the man there
asks them.

"Yes, yes," they say together.
"Show it to me," the man says.
They look at each other. Slowly
Alberto pulls a few coins from
his pocket and shows the inspector.
He looks frightened. I know it is
not enough money.

The interpreter leans over and whispers to the
inspector. I can't hear what he says. The
inspector nods and lets them through.

I lift my fingers to my mouth and whistle
loud, loud! Alberto and Rosa turn to look at me.
They laugh and wave.

> They [the inspectors] looked at
> me and at my husband and said,
> "Let them go through. They are
> young, they will make it! Don't
> worry about them."
> —Esther Almgren and her husband,
> who possessed $1.50 total,
> arrived from Sweden in 1923

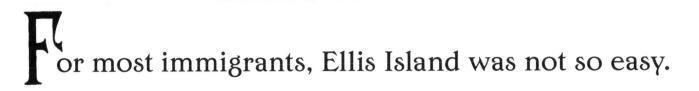

For most immigrants, Ellis Island was not so easy.

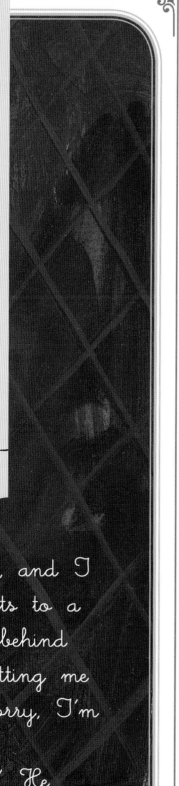

We could not let a woman with her children out on the streets looking for her husband. This also applied to all alien females, minors, and others who did not have money, but were otherwise eligible and merely waiting for friends or relatives. We generally had more of this class than we could handle. One Sunday morning, I remember, there were seventeen hundred of these women and children kept in one room with a normal capacity of six hundred. How they were packed in! It had to be seen to be appreciated.

—Frank Martocci, interpreter

"Little girl!" The interpreter's voice is loud, and I jump. "Go and wait over there." He points to a group at the side of the room. They are behind wire, like a cage, like a pen. Are they putting me in jail? Is it because I whistled? I'm sorry, I'm sorry, I won't make a sound!

"Go along!" he says. "Wait over there." He pushes me into the pen.

Not everyone was admitted. America wanted
the healthy and strong, people who could work,
people who would not need charity.

They detained my sister, who wore leg braces. She had polio as a child. My mother made her dresses a little longer, hoping they wouldn't notice, and they did. But my father [already in America] could prove that she would not be a burden to the country if they admitted her. So we just stayed overnight.
—Doris Fagendam
arrived from the Netherlands in 1908, age 10

While I believe that the coming here of all desirable immigrants should be facilitated, yet I am very emphatic in the belief that rigid means should be adopted to keep away those who are undesirable. . . . Last year over 2,000 cases of aliens who had arrived within the past twelve months, and in the meantime become destitute, were reported to the out-of-door poor department of the city of New York.
—William Williams,
commissioner at Ellis Island, 1902

Soon I am in a little room. There are more men to ask questions here, besides the one who tells me what to say. They do not wear uniforms, just suits. No one looks angry, but I am frightened, Mama.

"Now, little girl, what is your name?"

"Sera Assidian." My voice is small.

"And how old are you?"

I know it is wrong to lie. But I don't see Papa here to claim me, and I must come into America! What can I do? "Sixteen," I whisper.

"What year were you born?"

I remember that. "Three years after the year they burned Adana, the year they killed Grandfather and Grandmother."

The man says, "1896?" to himself. He looks at me, and his voice is very gentle. "So you were born around 1899 or 1900. Then you are not really sixteen, are you?"

I can barely breathe. "No," I whisper. "No, I am only ten." I hang my head.

He frowns. "What adult is with you?"

"Papa."

"Where is he? Did he travel with you?"

"No, no—he is here now, here in America." I choke a little. "My ticket—Papa paid my ticket."

"Where is your papa?" they ask me. Where? I take out the piece of paper and hand it to them. It is Papa's last letter to us, before the killings. It has his address on it.

"We will send him a telegram," one man says. "Don't be afraid. He will come for you tomorrow."

I sigh, closing my eyes, all the breath falling out of me.

Children could not pass through alone. Sometimes they had to wait for days until an adult already in the country came to meet them.

I waited for my father, but he never came. I was upset because I couldn't get off Ellis Island, because I didn't have enough money for them to let me off. In addition, I was not only an immigrant, I was a minor. But he came the next morning, a Friday.

—Samuel Silverman
arrived from Austria in 1913, age 15

A special woman talked to us in Greek and we felt more secure. We knew we were in the right place and that our father was going to come. And she told us, "Don't worry or cry. Your father is going to come—if not tonight, he will be here tomorrow. . . ."

—Bessie Spylios
arrived from Greece in 1909, age 11

When you went to sleep you were afraid that maybe somebody was going to come during the night and pull you out and say, "Well, you're sick. Come on, we'll send you back...." You lived in constant fear of being sent back.
—Regina Sass Tepper
arrived from Poland c. 1914

People who were waiting slept in dormitories. How crowded they were! Two small cots hooked together, with two more above them—and a couple feet away, another set of four cots, and another. It must have been hard to wait there, not yet in America.

They take me to a big room with many beds. I am so tired, I lie down and fall asleep. I even forget to say my prayers, Mama. Just this once. In the night I dream of home, of you smiling at me and singing a lullaby. Then the shots come, and I wake up screaming.

It is morning. No one is shot here. That was just my dream. I wash myself, I eat in the big dining hall, I walk outside. I wait for Papa. Soon we will be together in America, just like you told me.

Sera

Some of the people waiting were making an appeal. They had been turned away, and in a little courtroom, near the Great Hall, they were asking a special board of examiners to look at their case again, to let them come into America.

I've heard stories of the roughness [of the inspectors] . . . the roughness consisted of somebody who did not make it. That was tough. That was worse than killing them. But we had to be honest enough. We had to go by the law.
—Jacob Auerback,
immigration inspector

Several hundred immigrants daily were found to be suffering from trachoma, and their exclusion was mandatory. It was harrowing to see families separated. . . . Sometimes, if it was a young child who suffered from trachoma, one of the parents had to return to the native country with the rejected member of the family.
—Fiorello La Guardia,
interpreter, 1910–1912

Dear Mama,

It is many days now, Mama. Papa is still not here. I learn a little English from the guards.

"Papa, today?" I ask.

"Not yet," they say, "not yet." It is a long time.

Today a guard takes my hand and leads me out of the room. Is Papa here, I wonder? But he leads me to the dock and pins a tag on me. Other people are here with me, a family of Gypsies, a woman with a sick child. Everyone looks sad, so sad.

The interpreter speaks to me gently.

"We are sending you back," he says. "It is the law. A child cannot come to America alone."

They would promise to be good workers, good residents, if only they could come in to America.

The hearings are very emotional. The aliens didn't know what to expect. Suddenly they were standing before a judge, a panel of people who decided whether they entered the United States or faced deportation.

—Joseph Gallo,
immigration employee, 1947–55

We had witnessed some terrible things. As a child, I had witnessed two thousand or so Armenians burned alive in a church. We even heard their cries from where we were. And one woman tried to escape from that burning church. And, of course, there were Turkish soldiers outside who shot her. Sometimes I hear their screaming and shouting even now.
—Vartan Hartunian
arrived from Armenia c. 1911

Back? Back to Armenia? But they will kill me! I will be dead like you, Mama. I scream, long, high, and turn to run.

The guard catches me. They put me in the little boat, and it leaves the dock. Mama, help me! I will die if I go back, die like all the others. Mama, Mama, look down from the angels and help me, help me. I fall on the deck, sobbing.

How would I vote?

Let them come in!

One instance of his kindliness had to do with a Jewish orphan child who had been placed aboard ship for return to Russia. Within an hour after the ship had left the dock, a brother of the boy appeared at Ellis Island and convinced Mr. Watchorn that he could take care of him. The commissioner hurriedly boarded a tug, overhauled the ship, and brought the child back in his arms.

—R. Watchorn,
commissioner of Ellis Island, obituary

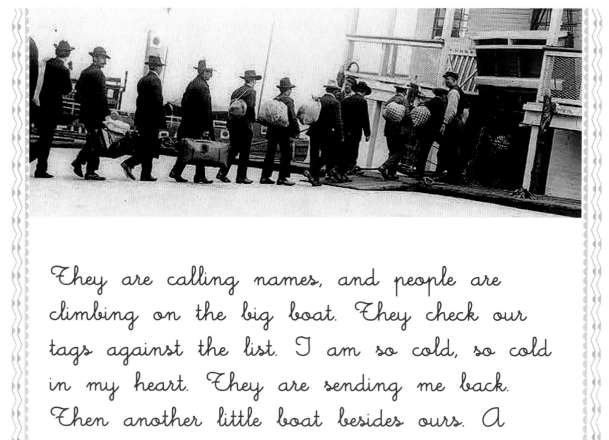

They are calling names, and people are climbing on the big boat. They check our tags against the list. I am so cold, so cold in my heart. They are sending me back. Then another little boat besides ours. A guard calls, "Sera Assidian!"

"That's me!" I cry. What is happening?

Outside the building a long, low wall, the Wall of Honor, curves around the shore. There are names, thousands and thousands of names, carved on it. The name of my grandmother's grandmother is here.

All of a sudden, my mother spotted him, spotted my father. She says, "It's Papa!" I looked. I had forgotten what he looked like, you know. He hugged me and patted me on the back.
—Mario Vina
arrived from Italy in 1909, age 11

They sent a telegram to my father, and he came the next day to get me. . . . It was the first time I ever saw him. And the officials would ask me questions, and then him questions, trying to determine if he was, in fact, my father because I didn't remember him. And then I guess they were satisfied, and they let me go with him.
—Cara Weichel
arrived from Austria in 1905, age 9

They put me on the other little boat. The man in a suit is there. "Your father has arrived," he tells me. "We'll meet him now."

In the big hall there is a man waiting. I look up at him. So tall! Is it Papa? I can't remember how he looks. Oh, Mama, how I wish you were here!

The inspectors ask him questions, and they look at papers. Then they smile. "Yes, this is your papa," they tell me.

I trace the chiseled words with my fingertip, feeling the cool stone, the sharp edges of the letters.

A young woman, only sixteen. She came here alone, among a crowd of strangers. Came into the unknown.

Mary. My grandmother's grandmother.

An American.

They were calling people who came to pick somebody up. And finally they called our name. . . . My father and my brother was there, and an uncle of mine. I remember my father putting his arms around my mother and the two of them standing and crying, and my father said to my mother, "You're in America now. You have nothing to be afraid of. Nothing at all." . . . That's the first thing he said to her.
—Esther Gidiwicz
arrived from Romania in 1905, age 5

"Sera?" He leans over and lifts me up, even though I am a big girl now, too big to lift like a baby. Then, suddenly, I remember. I remember Papa standing outside our house, lifting me in his big arms, high into the sky, and all around me the doves' wings fluttered like angels, and you were singing, Mama.

I remember.

"Papa!" I cry, hugging him, holding him. I am laughing, we are both laughing now. "Papa, I am in America!"

FURTHER SUGGESTED READING

BOOKS

Chermayeff, Ivan, Fred Wasserman, and Mary J. Shapiro. Ellis Island: An
Illustrated History of the Immigrant Experience. New York: Macmillan;
Toronto: Maxwell Macmillan Canada; 1991.

Jacobs, William Jay. Ellis Island: New Hope in a New Land. Atheneum: New York
City, 1990.

Yans-McLaughlin, Virginia, Marjorie Lightman, and The Statue of Liberty–Ellis
Island Foundation. Ellis Island and the Peopling of America: The Official
Guide. New York: New Press: Distributed by W.W. Norton, 1997.

WEBSITES

The National Park Service. "Ellis Island National Monument."
http://www.nps.gov/elis/

The Statue of Liberty–Ellis Island Foundation, Inc. "Ellis Island Passenger Arrivals:
American Family Immigration History Center." http://www.ellisisland.org/